Jean Gill

D1490304

Unless You Become Like a Little Child

Seeking the Inner Child
in Our Spiritual Journey

Paulist Press *New York/Mahwah*

Library of Congress
Catalog Card Number: 85-60415

ISBN: 0-8091-2717-2

Published by Paulist Press
997 Macarthur Boulevard
Mahwah, New Jersey 07430

Printed and bound in the
United States of America

Contents

Dedication

to my children
Kathy, Mary, John, Maureen, Theresa and Sharon

and my grandchildren
Michelle and Kevin

who show me the ways of a child

Acknowledgments

I am especially grateful to my family, friends and fellow travelers, who have walked with me on my journey, listened to my stories, and shared their stories with me. They have supported, encouraged and challenged me in many spiritual births, out of which were born this book.

Special thanks are due to those who reviewed the manuscript and gave me their valuable suggestions and comments. I owe particular thanks to my daughters Sharon and Theresa, who typed the manuscript.

My deepest gratitude goes to my husband Walt for his constant, loving companionship along the way, his enthusiastic support and encouragement, and his helpful suggestions.

My appreciation goes to Robert Hupka for his gracious assistance and for permission to use his photographs of the Pieta. Reprinted from *Michelangelo: Pieta* by Robert Hupka. Copyright 1975 by Robert Hupka. Used by permission of Crown Publishers, Inc. The book contains one hundred fifty photographs of the Pieta, with text in six languages.

The excerpt from "On Reason and Passion" is reprinted from *The Prophet,* by Kahlil Gibran, by permis-

Introduction

Unless you change and become like little children, you will not enter the kingdom of God (Matthew 18:3).

This familiar passage from Matthew's Gospel is a challenging call from the Lord. It summons us to a journey of exploration, a quest for the deeper meanings hidden beneath the words. It urges us to search for ways to respond to Jesus' challenge ever more fully. Sometimes we succeed in catching a glimpse of light. At other times we are left perplexed and baffled, sensing a deeper meaning beyond our grasp. There is a rich hidden treasure waiting to be discovered within each one of us. In order to find it, we need to turn our attention inward and focus on our spiritual journey—the journey in which we seek to enter the kingdom of God within.

On this journey there are many aspects or parts of our selves that can either help or hinder us along the way. Our inner child is a key figure who, like the other actors in this drama of our journey, can either facilitate or impede our progress. It is essential for us as travelers to tend to our child. A child ignored is a child who is likely to throw a tantrum or engage in any number of mischievous activities to try to gain attention. When that happens, we certainly do not get much accomplished. Instead, we are busy repairing the damage and replenishing our emotional energy. On the other hand, if we allow our inner child to be in charge, the results can get us seriously sidetracked from our journey. Children are notorious for becoming lost, so it would not be wise to depend on our child as a guide for our spiritual pilgrimage.

We need to care for our inner children in much the same ways that we care for physical children. We need to nurture and protect them, listen to them, accept, embrace, and love them as they are. Then they will bring joy and warmth to our inner journeys just as they do to our outer households. We will learn from them as they speak to us with the clear and refreshing wisdom that comes from the mouths of children in a special way. Jesus said: "Father, Lord of heaven and earth, to you I offer praise; for what you have hidden from the learned and the clever you have revealed to the merest children" (Matthew 11:25).

In this book we will explore the characteristics of a little child that are significant to the spiritual journey. We will look at some of the ways in which we can grow in love and understanding of our own inner child, and ways in which we can provide care and nurturing for this beloved little child. We will also consider some common barriers to this growth process.

I offer my hand in companionship and encourage-ment to those who want to embark on the spiritual journey and to those who are already well along the way in prayer and yearn to draw ever closer to the Spirit of God within.

I invite you to come with me . . .
    to ask the Lord to travel at your side
        as you journey inward
            in search of your child . . .
    to open your arms in love . . .
        to receive this precious child of yours
            deep into your heart . . .

to stand before God
    in your smallness . . .
        with your child's face turned upward
          to meet God's loving gaze . . .
and to run into God's outstretched arms . . .
    to become lost in God's joyful embrace . . .
    to become one with God in love.

1

Like a Little Child

Imagine two small children playing at the beach . . .
   a little boy and a little girl.
      Pretend that you are one of the children.

Be very still for a moment.
   Listen to the sound of the surf.
   Smell the ocean air.
   Look at the sky.
      Notice the color . . .
         and the presence or absence of clouds.
   Feel the air . . .
      warm or cool, breezy or still.

Crouch down and touch the sand.
   Notice how it feels . . .
      wet or dry, cool or warm.
   Let it sift through your fingers.
      Feel the tiny grains between your fingertips.
      Listen to the sound of the sifting sand.

Begin to build a castle with the sand.
   Feel the sand as you try to shape it.
      Become aware of your emotions . . .

as the sand yields to your touch . . .
as it collapses . . .
as you try again . . .
as the shape becomes pleasing
   or displeasing to you.

A wave comes close to your castle.
   The next wave reaches your feet.
      Feel the water . . .
         cold . . . cool . . . warm.
      Pay attention to your emotions . . .
         as each wave comes closer . . .
         as one wave finally reaches the castle
            and washes over it . . .
         and there is nothing left except
            a smooth place on the sand.

One of the children runs away from the water . . .
   and stands at a distance from it.
      The other stands at the water's edge.
   Be the child at the edge of the water.
      Feel the waves wash over your feet.
      Feel the sensation as the retreating waves
         pull the sand from under your feet . . .
            and it seems as if you are being drawn
               into the deeper water.
      How do you feel?
         Frightened? Excited? Adventurous?
         Confused? Curious?

Run away from the water
   and stand beside the other child.
      Watch the waves for a time.
         Become aware of your feelings.

Be the other child now.
   How do you feel?

Curious? Afraid? Adventurous?
Reach out and take the hand of the first child.
Together, go back to the water.
Feel the excitement and fear
mixed together . . .
as the sand shifts under your feet . . .
as you find the courage to stay . . .
as you discover that it is not
as dangerous as it seemed.
Begin to sense the friendliness . . . the playfulness . . .
the beauty of the water . . .
as you remember also its power . . .
its danger . . . its depth.

Slowly . . . hand in hand . . .
walk away from the water again.
Sit together at a distance.
Be still and sense the ocean.
Let its mystery fill you . . .
know its beauty . . . its danger . . .
its friendliness . . . its power . . .
its playfulness . . . its depth.

The deep waters of the sea are a common symbol of
our inner self. The spiritual journey is a voyage inward to
the depths of our being, to the still point where God is
profoundly present. From deep within our selves the still,
small voice of the Spirit calls us, beckoning us to enter
within, to be united with God in an intensely intimate and
loving relationship. The scene of the children at play by
the water suggests some of the characteristics of our inner
child which are significant to our inward, spiritual
journey.

The children stand at the meeting place between sea
and land, between our inner and outer selves. They have
conflicting emotions. Their curiosity and adventurous
spirits prompt them to wade into the deeper water. Their

fear of the power and darkness of the ocean inclines them to run away from the water. How we deal with our child-like feelings can have a great deal to do with whether or not we choose to step into the water and begin our spiritual journey in earnest and, once begun, whether or not we will persevere.

It is important to know and listen to our inner child. It is also important that we do not allow our child to be in charge of our decision-making process. If we act on our childlike impulses alone, we may plunge into the deep waters recklessly and dangerously, moved by curiosity and excitement. On the other hand, we may turn and flee in fear, unable to summon forth the courage to hear and follow the call of the Spirit from deep within our selves. We will explore in the next chapter some of the other aspects of our selves which we need to use in finding our way and in shaping our attitude toward our journey within.

First of all, though, it is of primary importance simply to get to know our inner child as well as we can. We need to accept and embrace our child within as a precious and lovable part of our selves, including those childish traits that do not seem very lovable. Only then can we develop the truly childlike attitude that is so vital in our relationship with God.

If we want to get to know a person better, we need to spend time together. The same is true of our inner child. We cannot achieve a closer relationship by simply thinking about it. We need to spend time with our child and we need to involve our emotions and our imagination during that time.

One exercise you might try would be to use the scene of the children at play by the water. Become comfortable and quiet and close your eyes. Then spend between twenty minutes and an hour in your imagination at the beach; pretend you are one or both of the children. Let your imagination go free, using the original scene simply as a starting point. Do whatever you feel like doing as a child at the beach. Pay very close attention to your emotions. If you notice a feeling beginning to surface, try to stay with it and allow yourself to experience it *as a little child.*

Music can be effective in providing a setting in which to spend time with our inner child. For example, "Swedish Rhapsody" by Alfven tends to evoke images of childlike activity and emotions. Just become quiet, pretend you are a child, listen to the music and let it lead your imagination freely. *La Mer* by Debussy can also be helpful, especially in light of our consideration of the ocean as a symbol of our interior depths. Again pretending to be a child, you could explore the surface and/or the depths of the sea, letting the music suggest the action of the water. The depths of the ocean can be very stimulating for our childlike curiosity. Old ruins and priceless treasures can be found at the bottom of the sea. Its darkness and its unfamiliar terrain can bring about many surprises, both wonderful and frightening. Our exploration and discoveries can call forth feelings of playfulness and joy as well as fear and anxiety. Pay close attention to any feelings that surface and, as before, allow your self to experience them as a child.

Any imaginative exercise that allows us to be like a little child can be helpful in breaking down the barriers that keep us from developing the spiritually childlike ways to which we are called by the Lord.

Jesus called for the children, saying: "Let the little children come to me. Do not shut them off. The reign of God belongs to such as these. Trust me when I tell you that whoever does not accept the kingdom of God as a child will not enter into it" (Luke 18:16–17).

2

The Divine Child

Silent night, Holy night,
All is calm, All is bright,
'Round yon Virgin Mother and Child,
Holy Infant so tender and mild.
Sleep in heavenly peace,
Sleep in heavenly peace.

Joseph Mohr/Franz Gruber

Imagine the familiar nativity scene portrayed by this traditional Christmas carol . . .

the infant Jesus lying in a manger . . .
Mary and Joseph close by . . .
the shepherds with their sheep . . .
the three wise men with their gifts
of gold, frankincense and myrrh . . .
the angels . . . the star.

Spend a few moments in silence to let the scene emerge in your imagination. Notice the sights . . . the sounds . . . the smells . . .

the feel of the wood . . . the straw . . .
the woolly coat of the lamb . . .
the infant's tiny hand.

Sense the atmosphere . . . the mood . . .
and any emotions it evokes from within your self.

The nativity scene can be viewed as an image of inner wholeness. It has a power to stir us to our depths, beckoning us toward the fullness of life which it portrays. Let us explore the picture from this point of view, looking at the individual figures and their relationships to the whole.

Looking at the scene from the inner perspective, we can view the Christmas story as taking place within our selves. Each figure in the scene becomes an image of a specific aspect of our selves which has an important part to play in our spiritual journey toward wholeness.

The nativity scene gives a general circular impression, with all the figures gathered around the infant Jesus at the center, like spokes converging at the hub of a wheel. The circle is a universal symbol of wholeness or fullness of life. Just as the infant Jesus is at the center of the circle, the Divine Child is at the center of our being—the image of God deep within each of us. The voice of the Spirit calls us constantly and insistently to bring to birth the divine life within. It is a lifelong process of many new births, as we discover and rediscover the divine within our selves. The position of the Divine Child at the center of the circle suggests the prominence of the role of our inner child on the spiritual journey. When we discover and embrace our inner child, we discover the Divine Child within—and we enable the birth of the divine life within our selves to continue. We will look now at the other figures in the scene, seeking to discover what part each plays in bringing to birth and nurturing the Divine Child within us—furthering our growth in holiness and wholeness of life.

Mary

Mary plays a major role in the Christmas story—and in the drama of our inner journey. To discover that role, we need to look at what she is like as the mother of the infant. We begin where her motherhood began—at the conception of the child, the annunciation (Luke 1:26–38). At the appearance and the greeting of the angel, Mary was "deeply troubled by his words, and wondered what his greeting meant." She surely felt surprised, confused, afraid. Upon the angel's announcement that she would conceive and bear a son, she was further confused. When told that "the Holy Spirit will come upon you and the power of the Most High will overshadow you," Mary responded with total acceptance: "Let it be done to me as you say."

Our inner Mary is like that. When we sense a significant communication from God, we are likely to feel emotions similar to Mary's—surprise, confusion, and fear. Like Mary, we need to hear the angel's calming and affirming voice, "Do not fear. . . . You have found favor with God." And then, in the midst of our confusion and inner turmoil, we need to accept from God the announcement that a new divine life is beginning within us. It is a crucial moment. We, like Mary, have a free choice. In order for the new life to take root and begin to grow, we need to accept the seed from God. The characteristics of Mary which we need at this beginning-time are *receptivity and openness* to God's creative touch, even when we do not understand it. For it is not understanding that is needed, but rather acceptance and surrender, allowing God to be the Lord of our life. Like Mary, we need the humility to say, "I am the servant of the Lord."

This is often an extremely difficult and critical experience of the spiritual journey. Like Mary, God calls us to move into a new and unexplored segment of our pilgrimage—to allow the beginning of a new birth of divine life within our self. It is our inner Mary who enables us to overcome our fears and to open our hearts and allow the seed of God's word to be implanted deep within the womb of our inner self, to take root and to flourish.

Let us now look at Mary as an expectant mother. She would surely experience the same emotions as any other pregnant woman: eagerness, anxiety, weariness, serenity, curiosity, and a feeling of being full of life. Our inner Mary is likely to experience similar emotions. Like Mary, we need to give the newness time to develop; we must wait for the coming-to-term of the infant. The characteristics of Mary which we need to foster during this time are *patience* and an attitude of *passive waiting*. We need to be patient with the process and patient with our selves as we go through the process. We cannot shorten the time through any effort on our part. We need to allow the new life to come to term according to God's time, our own inner "spiritual clock."

Mary's experience of the labor and birth of Jesus would also be similar to that of any other woman during childbirth, with the same mixture of emotions: excitement, fear, total absorption, physical pain and exertion during the labor; joy and ecstasy, relief and exhaustion after the birth. Mary would be involved differently during each stage of labor as any woman would. In the first stage of labor, a woman needs to relax and let go during the contractions. The second stage of labor is a transition time between the deliberate letting go of the first stage and the bearing down of the third stage. During the transition stage, a woman is likely to experience greater pain and a sense of confusion and helplessness. A feeling of panic is common at this time, a sense of being unable to endure the labor. Fortunately, this transition time is usually brief. A woman who has previously given birth can draw strength from the memory of the fleeting nature of this stage, and know that she can endure it again for that short time.

The third stage of labor is the actual birth of the child, and it is then that a woman can become actively involved. She can bear down with the contractions. She can significantly affect the process of bringing her child to birth. A woman can experience a feeling of great satisfaction in the midst of this hard work, being able at last to do something active and effective. One of the rare peak moments of a woman's life is very likely to be the moment of that final contraction when she bears down with what may seem to be her last bit of strength, and brings forth her own child into the world and into her arms. The characteristics of Mary which we need to cultivate during the labor and birth of the new life within our selves are: *letting go, endurance,* and *active involvement.*

After the birth there is a time of embracing the newborn child, resting, and nursing. Again, Mary would certainly experience most of the same mixed feelings as any new mother: joy, ecstasy, serenity, anxiety, confidence, a sense of fulfillment, fatigue, tenderness, impatience, and patience. The characteristics of our inner Mary which we need to encourage at this time are dispositions of *embracing* and *nurturing* the newness in our self.

The stages of a normal, full-term pregnancy and birth are universal, clear-cut and fairly predictable. The stages of our inner pregnancies are not usually so clearly defined; they have a tendency to be vague and overlapping. We tend to experience the same emotions as Mary, and our feelings are valuable clues to indicate that a process of spiritual birth may be occurring. But it is only through experience and careful discernment that we learn to recognize the stages of our own individual spiritual growth. When we do, then we can respond as Mary did, with the characteristic attitude appropriate to the specific stage of the process—and the new birth is encouraged and enabled to proceed. In summary, those responses are:

- receptivity and openness at the beginning;
- patience and passive waiting during the gestation period;
- letting go, endurance, and active involvement during the labor and birth;

- embracing and nurturing during the early life of our newborn inner child.

We often learn by trial and error. Being in touch with our emotions can help us to recognize an inappropriate response which will hinder the process of inner birth. For example, we may be "bearing down" during the first stage of our inner birthing process when we need to relax and let go. In a physical birth, this will increase the pain and impede the progress of labor. That is exactly the effect we are likely to feel in our spiritual labor if we are actively trying to control something in our life when it is time to let go. We feel increased pain and frustration in the situation. If we realize that and let go of our inappropriate attachment we usually feel the same effect that a woman in labor feels when she relaxes with the contractions: relief, a decrease in pain, and a sense that the birthing process is freed to proceed at the natural rate. We may also experience a time of panic, confusion and helplessness during the transition stage of our spiritual birthing. Like an experienced mother, we can call on our memory of previous inner births to assure our selves that this will pass and that we can endure it. We can also be comforted by the knowledge that soon we can do something active and concrete to bring about the birth of the new life within our selves.

We all have an inner Mary, whether we are men or women and whether or not we have physically given birth to a child. The spiritual birthing process can occur in all of us. We all need to develop Mary's feminine characteristics and respond as she did at each stage of the process in order for the birthing to proceed.

There is an interesting similarity between the French word for "sea," *mer,* and the French word for "mother," *mère.* It underscores the vital connection between the attributes of mothering and the ability to enter within our selves on the spiritual journey—remembering that the sea is a symbol of our inner depths.

We have given a good deal of attention to the role of our inner Mary in the coming to birth of the divine life within our selves. Because of her uniquely significant role in the process, we will return to her later in the book. For now, let us turn to the other figures in the Christmas story and continue the exploration of the parts they play in the drama of our journey.

Joseph

As with Mary, the most direct way to discover what Joseph is like is to focus on his emotions at key points in the story. We can identify our own inner Joseph through the feelings we have in common with Joseph in the Christmas story. This then leads us to the essential characteristics of his role in the scriptural narrative and in our own inner story.

When he learned of Mary's pregnancy, Joseph most likely experienced mixed feelings such as shock, hurt, rejection, anger, confusion, compassion, and finally decisiveness and relief. "Joseph her husband, an upright man unwilling to expose her to the law, decided to divorce her quietly" (Matthew 1:19). But then he had a dream in which he was told by an angel, "Joseph, son of David, have no fear about taking Mary as your wife. It is by the Holy Spirit that she has conceived this child" (Matthew 1:20). Joseph probably experienced emotions such as astonishment, apprehension, confusion, doubt, decisiveness and relief.

In the first instance, Joseph manifested characteristics of *objectivity, fairness,* and *decisiveness.* In acting on his dream, he demonstrated *trust in spiritual experiences* and *flexibility.*

During the journey from Nazareth to Bethlehem, the birth of Jesus, the flight into Egypt, and later the return to their home in Nazareth, Joseph must have had such feelings as protectiveness, a sense of responsibility, fatigue, and caring. He showed characteristics of *protectiveness, commitment,* and *decisiveness.*

The qualities exhibited by Joseph are vitally important to the birth, survival, and growth of the Divine Child within us. Especially important are *objectivity, fairness, decisiveness, trust in spiritual experiences (expressed by acting on them), flexibility, protectiveness,* and *commitment.* We can identify our own inner Joseph through the feelings we have in common with the Joseph of Scripture, as well as the characteristics shown by him in guiding, caring for, and protecting Mary and the child. We all have an inner Joseph, whether we are women or men. We need to encourage the development of these characteristics in order to be able to see our selves fairly and objectively, perceiving the guidance of the Spirit in our spiritual experience and acting decisively on that perception. We need to be protective of our new life as it emerges, not allowing outside (or inside) influences to harm it or to hinder its growth and development.

Jesus

Before we continue with the other supporting characters of the Christmas story, let us take a closer look at the central figure of the nativity scene, the infant Jesus. What was this newly experienced birth like for this tiny infant? It must have been filled with sharply contrasting feelings, just as it is for any child being thrust from the warm and sheltered environment of his mother's womb into the outer world. Certainly it was a traumatic experience. Jesus as an unborn child surely felt the warmth and security of his mother's womb, the steady, reassuring beat of her heart. Then came the disruption of the labor contractions—the pushing, pulling, squeezing during the birth. Then the passage through the birth canal into the cold air, feeling the open space, the loss of the secure support of the womb. Jesus as a newborn infant must have felt panicky as his arms and legs were suddenly freed, no longer touching the walls of his mother's womb, his familiar abode. He must have felt very frightened in this larger, unknown space, with this new freedom.

What was it like for this little baby to feel air in his lungs for the first time? To hear and feel the sound of his own first cry? So many traumatic new experiences in such an incredibly short time!

How must the infant Jesus have felt as he was wrapped in the soft, warm swaddling clothes for the first time? As he was held in Mary's arms and heard her familiar heartbeat again? As he was drawn to the comfort of her breast, as he nursed and felt the warm, sweet milk filling him with nourishment, satisfying his new hunger?

What was it like for Jesus to be held by Joseph? To feel his strong, firm, masculine embrace? How was it for this tiny infant to be thrust into this new and unfamiliar and frightening world—and then received into the soft, nourishing, feminine embrace of Mary and the firm, strong, masculine arms of Joseph? How peaceful and satisfied he must feel now, resting snug and warm in the manger. His sense of security must surely have been restored, as even now he begins to sense that Mary and Joseph will be nearby to care and provide for him in this new world he has entered.

Each time our own inner child comes to birth, the birth of the divine life within our selves is enabled to continue. During these spiritual births, we are likely to experience feelings and sensations similar to those just ascribed to the infant Jesus during birth, and they are valuable clues to indicate that a birth is in progress. We may feel a disturbance following a time of peace and security. There can be a traumatic leaving of a previous way and a seemingly violent thrust into new and unfamiliar ways. We may feel panic and fear, and a longing for security and comfort and nourishment. It is important to call on our own inner Mary and Joseph to receive and cherish, to nurture and protect this precious newborn child of ours.

The Shepherds and the Sheep (Luke 2:8–18)

When approaching the Christmas story from an inner perspective, the sheep and shepherds symbolize aspects of our selves. The sheep as an image of one such aspect could signify our natural "animal" instincts, our sensuality and sexuality, our earthiness, our emotions. We must be in touch with these facets of our selves to be truly whole. We must accept and embrace our sheep and cherish them as the precious gifts that they are. If we reject any part, we hinder our progress on the spiritual journey toward wholeness; we impede the birthing process.

The shepherds are earthy, simple, common-sense folk. They tend the sheep. They lead them to pastures where they can find nourishment. They protect them. They seek and find them when they wander away and are lost. They embrace them gently, returning them to the fold. They keep the sheep in bounds. We all have an inner shepherd who, when accepted and embraced, can tend to our sheep as a good shepherd would, with firm but loving care.

It was the shepherds, who are so closely in touch with the sheep, who first heard the good news of the birth and responded by going to find the Divine Child. We would be wise to be in touch with our inner shepherd, for it may be through our shepherd that we will first become aware of a new birth within our selves. For example, the surfacing of an unexpected feeling often calls our attention to a stirring of new life within.

The Wise Men (Matthew 2:1-12)

The three wise men, or astrologers, saw what few others saw. They followed the star and found the child. They looked at the infant Jesus and saw beyond the physical image to a profound spiritual insight. Their deeper vision was expressed by their gifts: gold, symbolizing royalty; frankincense, signifying divinity; and myrrh, foreshadowing suffering and death. They possessed keen awareness and insights. They were confident and able to rely on their vision to lead them to their goal.

We all have our inner wise men—a keen inner wisdom that can lead us to the Divine Child. We need to learn to trust our intuitions and insights—to take action and "follow our star" with confidence to find our child within.

Herod (Matthew 2:1-18)

Though not visible in the nativity scene, Herod plays an influential role in the Christmas story, and therefore in our own inner drama. He is implicitly present at the scene as an ominous threat to the infant. As king, he is in a position of power and control. He fears that his position is jeopardized by the appearance of the newborn king of the Jews. He feels afraid and angry, threatened by the imagined loss of power.

We all have an inner Herod, and we would do well to be wary of him. He symbolizes our resistance to the new life within, a feeling of losing control and a desire to hold on to the familiar and the known. Fear is the dominant force behind our resistance—often a fear that is unconscious and therefore even more powerful in its influence on us. Our inner Herod in his fear will attempt to kill the newborn divine life within, manifest in one way by our attempts to suppress or ignore the new life until it dies from neglect.

In a sense, our inner Herod is valuable to us in that he makes us uncomfortable through our fear, calling attention to our emerging newness. We need only to take care that Joseph and our wise men pay attention to their dreams and therefore know the danger and can escape Herod's wrath and save the child.

The Angels (Luke 2:8–15)

The angels are the spiritual messengers of God. They signify our own angelic capacity—our ability to communicate with God, to know God intimately. Our inner angel is our capacity for deep spiritual experience—the mystic in all of us.

Often this is the figure we find the most difficult to accept and embrace as a part of our self. A little voice within seems to say, "Who am I to think I could be that close to God?" It seems too lofty. We experience a false humility. It is very easy to deny the existence of our angel within, and to turn a deaf ear to that still, small voice of the Spirit calling unceasingly to each one of us from our depths . . .

to come ever closer . . .
to taste the sweetness of God's longing for us . . .
to be blinded by the light of God's vision for us . . .
to be consumed by the fire of God's passion for us . . .
to allow our hearts to be pierced . . .
to be opened and emptied, and then
to be filled to overflowing
with God's life and love poured out to us.

You may wish to spend some time becoming better acquainted with some or all of the characters in the Christmas story. You could spend several prayer periods living the story in your imagination. You might choose a scene from the story and use the full range of your senses to be as fully present there as possible. Take the role of one of the characters, or speak with·him or her, or just be with them. Perhaps touch his face or hold her hand or carry the infant Jesus or the small lamb. You might find it helpful to write out a dialogue. Be sure to pay careful attention to any emotions that surface; they can reveal much to you about your relationship to that part of your self.

Our inner relationships with the various parts of our self are similar to our relationships with other people. They are constantly changing. They are also subject to the disruptions that occur in outer relationships—the discomfort or fracturing that causes us to pay extra attention to that relationship, to heal it and come to an even closer union. Spending time in prayer experiencing the dynamics of our various inner relationships can reveal fragmentations and offer us the opportunity for healing and coming to greater wholeness.

3

The Child in Light

When we look at a little child, most of us can see numerous characteristics that are very appealing to us. When we see these attractive qualities, we are looking at the light or bright side of the child. We each have within our selves a little child with all of these delightful characteristics—a child who yearns to run along beside us as we travel the road of our spiritual journey.

Our inner children long for
the sight of our faces close to theirs . . .
the look of love in our eyes
as we gaze on them with our full attention . . .
the warmth and security of our embrace
as we gently draw them close to our selves . . .
the clasp of our hand
as we encourage them to accompany us
on our journey.

Sometimes our inner child feels starved for our attention, or seems dead for lack of our life-giving care and nurturing. Our little child may at times need to be brought back to fullness of life and vitality within our selves, to be led out of darkness back into the light.

Let us look at some of the appealing characteristics of our child in light, as well as some ways in which we may at times neglect to nurture and cherish these aspects of our child. These are qualities which are vital to our spiritual growth and need to be brought ever more fully into the light of awareness.

The first of these characteristics is a childlike *openness:*

- a sense of wonder and awe at all that life offers;
- an adventurous spirit that constantly explores;
- a curiosity that delights in discovering surprises;
- an insatiable desire to learn from life.

The development of an open attitude toward life helps us to accept life's experiences as valuable gifts and to learn from all of them, the way a child does—willingly exploring painful or disturbing events as fully as joyful or peaceful experiences. It is desirable to reach within and take the hand of our little child, who can lead us to explore life's painful experiences as openly as its joyful events. If an experience causes us pain, we can learn from it together, as a child learns something about fire after being burned. The child acquires a healthy respect for the power of the fire, and in time learns how to put that power to good use. It is important to feel the pain fully with our child, for it is the pain itself that teaches. If we were not burned and did not admit the hurt, the power of the fire could not be discovered—for it is the "burning" property of fire that is the source of its power.

An open attitude is like an open door—a welcoming, hospitable disposition toward the various travelers who come our way seeking to be admitted into our life. The travelers are our life experiences. They come clothed in various ways. To be hospitable is to welcome all who come, not turning aside those who look dirty or bedraggled or even threatening. Our experiences often come unbidden, and we are sometimes inclined to shut the door and to try to close out those that are disturbing. Yet it is these uninvited and unappealing travelers who are quite likely to carry a precious gift hidden under their dirty cloaks. A little child is inclined to let in anyone who comes to the door. We need to overcome our revulsion and fear and stand beside our own inner child to invite these travelers into our lives with a welcoming embrace. If we leave them outside at the fringe of our consciousness, we will not be able to receive the treasure they bear. We need to take them in and live with them for a time before the precious gift they carry is revealed to us.

Our spiritual life is like our external life in this regard. We may find that we are inclined to turn away from a disturbing feeling arising during our prayer time, or from a change in our usual way of prayer. A disturbing or painful spiritual experience usually presents us with an opportunity for new growth. We may feel an urge to close our spiritual door to such an experience out of fear of the ugliness or the unknown. Our ability to develop an open, welcoming attitude toward our prayer experiences helps us to develop the same attitude toward our outer experiences. Increasingly, we are able to welcome all of life with childlike eagerness and curiosity, exploring it as deeply as possible, discovering and receiving with open arms the precious gifts that our gracious and loving God is constantly offering to us.

Openness also includes being willing to perceive life with all of our faculties, not just our physical senses. For example, the use of our imagination is a childlike ability which is very important in prayer. Deeply significant spiritual experiences are often expressed in images. If we are accustomed to verbal or reflective forms of prayer, we may sometimes need to consciously let go of praying in those ways in order to develop our ability to use our imagination. Imagery is less predictable; it is often spontaneous and unplanned. Because of its spontaneous quality, the imagination has a unique value in revealing to us something that we may not have been consciously aware of. It allows us to perceive the movements of the Spirit at a deeper level. It is an exploration of unknown spiritual territory. Because of this, it often takes some courage to let go of our accustomed way of prayer and be open to using our imagination. We can take the hand of our child within who, with a childlike sense of adventure, will eagerly accompany us as we venture forth into this unknown region.

Paying attention to our dreams is a childlike kind of spiritual activity that is closely related to using our imagination. Our dreams are also unpredictable and spontaneous, and can reveal important insights from deep within our selves. It can be especially valuable to continue a significant dream in our imagination during our prayer time. This can be very effective in discovering the meaning of the dream. We can consciously re-enter the dream at any point we choose. We can ask questions, confront an attacker, make friends with an enemy, or whatever our imagination suggests. Our inner child stands ever ready and eager to accompany us in the adventure of exploring our dreams. An excellent guidebook for the exploration of dreams is *Dreams and Spiritual Growth: A Christian Approach to Dreamwork,* by Louis M. Savary, Patricia H. Berne, and Strephon Kaplan Williams (Paulist Press, 1984).

While openness is a childlike quality that is appealing to most of us, it often takes courage and determination to allow it to develop within our selves at ever deeper levels. As we grow in openness, we see ever more clearly that God not only loves us with a total and passionate love, but delights in surprising us with unexpected discoveries along our journey—and we may find our selves squealing with delight like a little child opening the gift of a new toy.

The second childlike characteristic we will ponder flows naturally from openness and is closely related to it. This second trait is *trusting dependence*. The helplessness of a baby or small child is an endearing quality. The image of an infant being held in the arms of a loving mother or father is one that has great appeal for most of us. There are times when we our selves feel just that helpless—confused, overburdened, lost and unable to find our way. We need to allow our selves to be gathered into the arms of God, to acknowledge our total dependence on God as our Father or Mother. However, it is often quite unappealing to us to view our selves as such a helpless infant. We may encounter strong resistance to becoming like a little child in this way. A voice within may be saying, "I should be able to control this situation, or to find an answer, or to be in charge of my life at all times." Paradoxically it is often only after we give up, acknowledge our helplessness, and surrender our selves into God's arms that we are able to go where God is trying to lead us. Only then are we truly in charge of our lives.

With each such experience, our trust in God can grow and we can surrender to God at ever deeper levels of our being. We can become ever more aware of how well we fit into the circle of God's arms as a little child, depending completely on God for care and guidance and for our very life.

Playfulness is the third characteristic we will explore. The word "playful" is likely to evoke a picture of children skipping, running or jumping with carefree abandon. We might also imagine a child deeply silent, totally absorbed in the wonder of a sea shell or a rock or a caterpillar, or creating a work of art with clay or sand or paint. In allowing our selves to be playfully childlike, we nurture our ability to be totally abandoned and absorbed in wonder and awe in the present moment. There is a deep letting go involved. We let go of our concerns about the past and our plans and visions for the future during the time that we are playing. We are free of cares for a time. Something wonderful can happen. Our creativity is released. Something inside lets go and we experience a great freedom. The Spirit of God is set free and is at play within us!

It is desirable to devote at least a portion of our prayer time to "playful" kinds of prayer that encourage the development of our ability to be totally absorbed in the present moment, carefree and open, allowing God to shape us from within. These include the simple forms of prayer in which we focus our attention on our breathing, our body sensations, the sounds around us, or perhaps a concrete object. We set aside for the time our thinking and our imagining.

An excellent source of guidance and specific exercises in this type of prayer is *Sadhana: A Way to God,* by Anthony deMello, S.J. (The Institute of Jesuit Sources, 1978, and Image Books, Doubleday & Co., Inc., 1984). The author presents exercises not only in the simple awareness forms of prayer, but also in the use of fantasy or imagination, as well as a section on the prayer of the heart, which he calls devotional prayer. There is such variety and richness in the exercises in *Sadhana* that it could serve as a resource for a lifetime of prayer.

"Playful" prayer also includes gestures, body movements, and dance, as well as free-form types of art such as clay sculpture and painting. These prayer activities can be highly effective in bringing us in touch with our inner child. Prayer might be described very simply as *spending time with God.* We grow closer to another person by spending time together in a variety of ways, and the same is true of God. Childlike ways of spending time with God can enrich and enliven our prayer time. We can discover a new delight in being with God in prayer.

As adults, we are likely to feel very inhibited in using these playful forms of prayer. One common source of inhibition is that we approach it as an adult, rather than as a child. A little child who is presented with a lump of clay for the first time is not likely to pose such adult questions as: What am I supposed to do with this?

Are there any special tools I should use?

What if my sculpture doesn't look as good as someone else's?

What if I don't feel inspired?

Where can I find the nearest class on clay sculpture?

If we are to reach out to God through the clay, and allow God to touch us through the clay, we must put aside such adult concerns and truly play with it as a child. A child would simply pick up the lump of clay and begin to discover what it is like and what can be done with it. The child has no plan for making a statue or any special shape. The child will simply become absorbed in the process— and that is precisely the purpose of using the clay in prayer. The purpose is not to produce anything, but to spend time absorbed in play with God.

Our use of gestures or dance or painting in prayer needs to be approached in the same childlike way as the clay. We need to avoid planning the body movements or worrying about our awkwardness, but rather let the music suggest the next movement. Likewise, we can let the paint and brush suggest the next stroke, simply being absorbed in the process of childlike discovery. In this simple, childlike play the Spirit of God is set free to move within us in a new way.

Let us turn our attention to a fourth childlike quality that is also vital to our spiritual journey. We will look at the characteristic of *growth* as an important childlike process. It is delightful to watch a child growing and learning new skills. Imagine a little girl learning to crawl. We can usually see some signs indicating that she is almost ready. She shows her desire to move by the look of excitement on her face, as well as her kicking and cooing, as she sees a brightly colored toy beyond her reach. She reaches out toward the toy but cannot touch it. She whimpers in frustration. She scoots and wiggles awkwardly and haphazardly, and sometimes succeeds in reaching the toy. She gurgles with satisfaction and plays happily with it for a time, until she spots another toy beyond her reach, and then she tries again. Suddenly one day, her arms and legs work together in coordination and she crawls to her toys. She is a bit awkward at first, but very quickly she is happily and skillfully crawling all around the house at quite a fast clip, leading her parents on a merry chase!

The child's parents cannot speed up the learning process, even though they might like their little girl to crawl sooner. When the time comes and they see that she is almost ready, however, they can encourage her by placing attractive toys just beyond her reach. They can love her when she fails and when she succeeds. They can provide opportunity and space for her to practice. But they cannot choose the time. Their little girl will crawl when her motor abilities are sufficiently developed and coordinated, and when the desire awakens within her. She will crawl when the time is right according to her own unique pattern of growth, and when the opportunity is present.

Each stage in a child's development progresses in a similar way. There is a period of approaching the point of readiness for the new skill. When that time is reached, a child typically experiences a feeling of restlessness, and begins to desire something new, though not knowing quite what it is nor how to achieve it. Then when the opportunity is present, there is the time of learning, which is often awkward and frustrating. The learning period is followed by the integration of the new skill, with a sense of accomplishment and elation.

Our spiritual growth as children of God is similar to the physical growth of a child, progressing in stages. Within each stage, there is a period of growing readiness. When the time of a new awakening approaches, we are likely to feel restless. Like a little child, we feel a desire to reach beyond where we are. Sometimes our longing is urgent and painful. We have a deep sense that the time is near, though this sense may be as yet unconscious and experienced only in our vague restlessness and desire.

32

Childlike, we do not know quite what the newness is, yet we reach out. Our urgent desire can be a surfacing of our deep longing for God and our reaching out for a new way of drawing closer to God.

We need to be like caring parents toward our little child within. We need to watch for and remove any obstacles or restrictions that may hinder us. We need to love our child as the new ability develops naturally in time. We especially need to be patient and loving of our selves as we flop on our face in childish awkwardness and frustration during the learning process.

One common way in which we may hinder our own growth toward God is to decide for our selves the best way and the best time for us to move. What does a child who has never yet crawled know about how to get to her toys? Likewise, what do we as little children before God know about how to move closer to God, and what should come next in our spiritual development? God will draw us ever closer in the ways of the Spirit which are yet to be revealed to us. God will show us the way. We need only to allow the process to unfold naturally and gracefully, letting God be the Lord of our journey. We can allow God to lead us by the hand like a little child and to continue to create us according to God's own vision of who we can be.

The fifth childlike characteristic we will consider is that of being *in touch with our feelings.* A child responds easily and naturally to feelings as they surface, and expresses them freely. We often look with delight on such spontaneity. As we mature, we learn to control our response to our feelings. Unfortunately, most of us also learn to ignore or suppress some of the feelings themselves. We learn that we shouldn't feel angry, or afraid, or jealous, or sexy, or any other feeling that is difficult to handle or causes discomfort. In so doing, we lose touch with our feelings and bury them away, out of sight. We lose our childlike ability to feel deeply, to experience life fully. We need to accept and embrace wholeheartedly this keenly sensitive inner child, so that we can learn again to recognize and to express all of our feelings, appreciating them, as precious signs of our selves as unique individuals.

Our prayer time can be an excellent opportunity to come into contact with our deepest feelings. We can simply focus our attention on whatever feelings are surfacing at the moment. Feel them as fully as possible, becoming like a child. Allow them to increase in intensity, or ebb and flow as they will. Tell the Lord in words how you feel. Or express your feelings in body movements or gestures, in clay or paint or crayon. Or imagine what the feelings are like. For example, feeling rejected by a friend may be like being locked outside of a house while that friend and others are having a party inside. It could be like sitting outside on the doorstep sobbing like a little child. We might feel like playing a trick on those inside to spoil their party and get even with them for our injured feelings. Then we might run into the open arms of God as our loving Father or Mother, crying and blurting out our story. We can receive comfort and consolation, and become lost in God's embrace.

It is not always easy to reveal our feelings to God like this, showing our selves just as we are. We may find it difficult or impossible to be so exposed. It may seem that God cannot love us as much if we reveal our childish anger or fear or desire to get even. Our reluctance comes ultimately from our inability to trust completely in God's total and unconditional love for us—a love that accepts and cherishes us just the way we are at any given moment, no matter how we are feeling or what horrible thing we think we have done. Being unable or unwilling to tell God how we really feel in prayer can be a stumbling block on our spiritual journey. We need to summon up our courage and take the risk in order to experience our selves as a little child secure in God's loving embrace.

The final childlike characteristic we will explore is that of being *in touch with our body.* Children are keenly aware of their bodies. They are in touch with the messages their bodies send to them, and they respond spontaneously with their bodies to emotional and physical stimuli. A hungry infant cries and kicks. A child recoils and howls from a puppy's nip. A toddler taking a first step may laugh aloud with delight. My granddaughter Michelle, at age two, provided me with a striking example of how easily and naturally young children can perceive body messages and integrate them into their experiences. A sudden noise startled her. She jumped, and then she put her hand on her stomach and said, "That scared me!" As we grow in age and maturity, we learn a valuable discipline of our body's responses. We learn to confine our physical reactions to appropriate times and places. Unfortunately, in the process of controlling the reactions, we sometimes lose touch with the body messages themselves. We fail to pay attention to them. For example, when our stomach tightens up, we may wonder if we ate something that disagreed with us. We would do well to listen more attentively to our stomach and ask our selves if there is something in our life we cannot "stomach." We could end up with an ulcer through our failure to attend to that question.

It can be worthwhile to reflect on our attitude toward our own body, to seek to discover what our relationship is with this very important part of our self. It would be valuable to know, for example, whether we see our body as a help or a hindrance—or as a prison or an integral part of our self that can be a true outer expression of our inner self. Most of us are probably somewhere between those extremes. One helpful way to discover how we perceive our body is to write out a dialogue with it, telling our body what we think and feel about it and writing out its replies. Our body is a valuable channel to our inner self, a medium through which God can speak to us from our depths. Our body often senses the Spirit's gentle voice long before our conscious mind is aware of the stirring.

Our emotions and our body sensations are similar in this way. They are both symbolized by the sheep of the nativity story who, with the shepherds, were the first to hear of the birth of the Divine Child. We need to attend carefully to our bodies as well as to our emotions if we wish to be in close touch with the Spirit of God within our selves and to grow in an ever more intimate relationship with God.

It is important to pray as a body-person. If we fail to integrate our bodies into our prayer, we hold back a part of our selves from God. There are many ways to incorporate our bodies more fully in prayer. Simply becoming aware of our breathing or posture or physical sensations is one way. A still but alert position can express our waiting and listening for God. Opening our hands can help us to be more open to God. Gesturing or dancing can enable us to express our selves to God in a way that words or images cannot.

Being in touch with our bodies and being playful are closely related. Playfulness is usually associated with running, jumping, and dancing—very physically childlike activities. Allowing our entire body to be involved in our prayer can be a wonderfully rich communication with God. It can help us to develop the valuable qualities of letting go and abandonment that are associated with playfulness. Bodily expression can bring a touching and releasing of deep spiritual experience, adding a new dimension to that of words, thoughts, feelings, and images. For example, our grief and repentance, our joy and ecstasy, our pain and anger, our praise and thanksgiving can be expressed in a unique way through body postures and movements. It is well worth overcoming any feelings of foolishness or clumsiness in order to discover a new dimension in our relationship with God. We can pray and play before God like a little child, and allow our experience of God as our loving Mother or Father to grow ever deeper.

We have explored six childlike characteristics: *openness, trusting dependence, playfulness, growth,* and *being in touch with our feelings and with our bodies.* Taken together, these six traits suggest a common quality that is typically found in little children: *simplicity.* Simplicity goes hand in hand with *humility.* To be simple and humble is to know our selves as we truly are, not as others think we should be, or as we think we should be or would like to be. It is to be fully our selves as truly as we are able and to live our lives accordingly. This is a lifelong task of the spiritual journey.

The call of God in our journey is a simple one. We are asked to trust and follow God as a loving parent who will:
take our hand and show us the way,
protect and guide us at every step,
provide us with abundant nourishment and care,
and love us with an everlasting, unconditional love.

God's way is simple, but it is not always easy. God calls us through death to new life, over and over again, beckoning us to ever deeper trust. Each time we abandon our selves into God's arms, we come closer to being able to accept God's inconceivably great love for us. We experience with ever deepening awareness the warmth and security of God's love and guidance.

Jesus is our model of this simple, humble, childlike way toward union with God. He showed us the way throughout his life, and his attitude is expressed powerfully and concisely during his agony in the garden and at the moment of his death. As he prayed in the garden the night before he died, he experienced intense fear in anticipation of the painful death he knew must be ahead for him. He addressed God as Abba, meaning daddy or papa, and evoking an image of a small child in the lap of a loving father. He said, "Abba (O Father), you have the power to do all things. Take this cup from me. But let it be as you would have it, not as I" (Mark 14:36). As he hung dying on the cross, he called out in his pain and terror, "My

God, my God, why have you forsaken me?" (Mark 15:34). And yet, even in the depths of his feelings of abandonment, Luke's Gospel tells us that as he breathed his last he spoke: "Father, into your hands I commend my spirit" (Luke 23:46). His final act in his physical life was an act of total surrender to his Father, Abba, and this in the midst of feeling abandoned by God. It is this surrender to which we are called on our journey toward union with God. We are called to the simple childlike trust that resurrection will follow after each surrendering death—that new life will come each time we let go and die to one of our old ways and open our selves to a new but unknown way toward which God is leading us.

We have considered six childlike characteristics that are vital to our spiritual growth, along with the common quality of simplicity. Our prayer time can provide a nurturing environment for the development of these childlike traits. By simply and humbly spending time with God as a child in prayer, we gradually can take on an overall childlike attitude in all of our life, and thereby enter ever more deeply into the kingdom of God within our selves.

4

The Child in Shadow

Just as we find a number of attractive qualities in a little child, so also most of us are aware of childish traits that are unattractive or unacceptable to us, even disgusting or repulsive. We tend to call these unappealing qualities childish, in contrast to the more attractive qualities, which we call childlike. When we see one of these unappealing traits shown by a child, we may find it difficult or impossible to feel loving toward the child at that time. When our inner child exhibits one of these childish characteristics, we may have a very difficult time accepting and embracing and loving that part of our selves. In other words, when we feel or think or behave "childishly," we may not be able to accept and love our selves. In fact, we would like to have that childish characteristic disappear, denying that it exists in us—simply blocking it out of our consciousness, relegating it to darkness and oblivion. This is the shadow side of our inner child. It is that side of our selves that we do not want to see, and so we often unconsciously close our eyes and pretend it is not there.

Our child in shadow does not cease to exist simply by being out of our sight. In fact, the inner child behaves in much the same way as an unsupervised physical child might: getting into mischief, cluttering and damaging the house, perhaps even injuring a pet or another child. An inner child in shadow is undisciplined and dangerous. We need to look at and deal with the shadow child, not close our eyes to it. We need to admit our childish tendencies and learn to deal with them constructively, consciously "supervising" them with our eyes wide open. These tendencies do not go away simply because we close our eyes to them; instead, they gain strength and run rampant. Then, blindly and unconsciously, we can harm our selves and others. Our inner child becomes autonomous, or outside of our conscious control, in proportion to the degree of our blindness.

Let us look now at some of the more common qualities which are part of the inner child in shadow for many of us. We have already touched on one of these characteristics which is often partly in shadow—our emotional child. We tend to pick and choose the feelings that are acceptable to us. We are willing to acknowledge and express the acceptable feelings, but we may repress the unacceptable ones. We may be unwilling to admit, for example, that sometimes we feel like a furious or confused or terrified or helpless child. Our idea that any specific feeling is unacceptable is usually rooted in our childhood. For example, someone may have said, "You shouldn't be angry," or "It is a sin to be angry." If we really believe that, then we are very likely to deny that we feel anger, while in fact we may be actually seething inside. Such repressed anger is a common experience for many of us, and it can be a formidable barrier on our spiritual journey. It merits some special attention.

How can we bring our anger into the light and deal with it? First of all, we need to believe that it is all right to feel angry, even to feel hateful and vengeful. It is our response to our anger that can be destructive and wrong. There are many constructive ways to deal with anger. We need to find an appropriate way for each individual situation, but first we need to recognize and feel our anger.

One good way to do this is to imagine our selves, perhaps as a child, describing our feeling to our selves or to God or to the person who is the object of our anger, even if it is God at whom we are angry. It often happens that as we begin to describe our feeling, we find it is much more intense than we thought. We may find our selves furious, or flying into a rage, throwing a tantrum, or thinking of a horrible punishment to inflict on the object of our fury.

A constructive and harmless way to express anger at this point is to imagine carrying out that tantrum or inflicting that punishment until the anger is spent. We may be horrified at the depth of our anger and at the fiendish punishments we can imagine. It is better that we know our potential for violence than that we blind our selves to it. For if we do not consciously see and supervise our angry inner child, then we are very likely to inflict our vengeance with a "cutting" remark or a "cold freeze" and then wonder, "What ever got into me?" On the other hand, instead of "murdering" in fantasy the person at whom we are angry, we may "kill" our selves slowly with an ulcer or some other physical ailment. If we act out our revenge in our imagination, we are less likely to act it out externally. Rather, it allows us to acknowledge and dissipate our anger without harming our selves or others.

When we deal with anger in our imagination, we are likely to feel very childish as we begin to get in touch with it and to feel its intensity. It can be very helpful to deliberately imagine our selves as a child and show our anger in childish ways. A story from my own spiritual journey may be helpful as an illustration.

About a year or so ago, during my prayer time, I realized I was angry with God. It was a feeling that had been slowly surfacing for several weeks. It was an anger that I had repressed for over twenty years—anger over the death from leukemia of my oldest daughter, Kathy, at the age of five. In my imagination I saw God sitting cross-legged on the floor across from me, with his arms open to me. I felt distant from him, ashamed of my anger and afraid to tell him how I felt. As I sat across from him, I felt smaller and smaller, until I was like a little child. I was ashamed to look at his face and could not go to him. I felt my anger growing. Finally, I blurted out something like: "It's not fair! You never asked me! You just took her away!" I sat there crying and raging and frustrated. God just sat there in the same loving and accepting way with his arms open. My anger and frustration increased and I threw my self down on the floor and had an all-out tantrum. I beat my fists and my feet on the floor and cried in rage until finally the anger was spent. I lay there, face downward, afraid to look at God. I wondered if he was still there and if he was now angry with me. Finally, I risked a quick peek. He was there, with his arms still open in loving invitation. After a long moment, I crawled over to him and into his lap, where I cried softly as he hugged me in an incredibly warm and loving embrace. The distance between us was dissolved. My twenty-year-old wound was healed and I was back where I belonged—a little child in God's arms.

I was surprised at my anger and at the childish feeling that God "took" Kathy from me. I thought I had discarded that concept of God as a distorted one. It was only in allowing my anger to surface, and letting my inner child blurt out her feelings, that the long-standing wound was exposed: I had discarded that concept of God from my head but not from my heart. Now in my prayer the healing could be completed, and I could know God more clearly, with my heart, as my loving Father who is always there to comfort and love me no matter what pain, or joy, or confusion I find in my life.

It is only after anger has been dealt with that reconciliation and forgiveness can begin. A wound cannot heal when it is being constantly irritated. Neither can a fractured relationship be healed until the aggravation of anger is removed. Forgiveness is critically important on our spiritual journey toward wholeness—forgiveness not only of others who have hurt us, but also forgiveness of our selves. Inner and outer forgiveness go hand-in-hand. We cannot forgive others until we have first forgiven our selves—until we have accepted and embraced our errant shadow-child.

Another emotion which is often hidden in the shadow side of our inner child is fear. Like anger, fear can also be a significant obstacle on our journey if we fail to acknowledge and deal with it. We are sometimes reluctant to admit to our "childish" fears. We think we "should have outgrown all that by now." We tend to feel like a foolish and helpless child when we catch a glimpse of a surfacing fear.

The reality is that fear is a human emotion that will surface regularly in the life of any person who is open and growing and traveling the road of the spiritual journey. It will almost surely appear each time our journey takes us to the frontier of new and unexplored territory. It is our fear of the unknown. It causes a normal and natural resistance in us—the sign that a new birthing process is about to begin. We need not be afraid to be afraid. We often need courage simply to acknowledge that we are afraid. Then we need further courage to allow the fear to surface, to experience it fully, and to attempt to see what we are afraid of.

A good way to get in touch with and begin to deal with our fear is to consider it during a quiet prayer time alone. Perhaps we are not even aware that we are afraid, but only that we are disturbed, or that something is bothering us. We can usually identify fairly easily what it is that is bothering us, and frequently it is a disturbance in our relationship with another person. We have a tendency then to begin to talk to our selves about the situation. Perhaps we defend our selves, or else we engage in an imaginary conversation with the other person as we try to find a way to resolve the problem. We are likely to find our selves talking in circles and getting nowhere. When that happens, we have probably taken a short-cut and we have gotten lost. We have skipped an important step.

What we need to do first is to identify our feelings. We often have mixed emotions. Perhaps we feel hurt, angry and afraid; this is a common combination. If someone has hurt us, it is a normal reaction to feel angry and vengeful. Underneath it all, we may be afraid of losing the love or friendship of the other person. We may be afraid of what she or he may think of us. The important question to ask at this point is, "What exactly am I afraid of?" It may take some time to answer that question, and it will also take some courage. As we begin to get closer to our fear, we are likely to begin to feel childlike, confused, helpless. Most of us resist those feelings, at least at first. More courage is needed to allow our selves to be childlike, and to stay with our fear, letting it surface and feeling its intensity. It can be tremendously helpful to call on Jesus to be with us. We can reach up and put our child's hand in his and allow him to protect and guide us. He may show us what we need to see. He may comfort us in our tears and inspire us with the courage to continue. Attempting to describe our fear to him may help to identify it more clearly. Naming our fear does not necessarily diminish it. It does clarify the situation so that we can decide freely how to act. A good question to ask at this point is, "What is the worst thing that could happen, and could I deal with it?" Courage is not the absence of fear. It exists alongside of fear and it means acting in spite of fear.

As we move deeper and deeper within our selves on our spiritual journey, our fears are deeper also. We may sense a vague foreboding that defies our attempts to name it. It arises as we begin to move into a new area of our spiritual growth, often before we are conscious of the movement. It may be expressed in a dream image or it may arise during a fantasy of our imagination. It could surface as an unexpected fear as we are praying with a Scripture passage. For example, we may find that we are afraid to ask Jesus to heal our blindness or our deafness, or that we are afraid to follow him up the road to Jerusalem, or any of an unlimited number of rich images from Scripture. What is needed is to stay with the fear and to avoid denying or repressing it. Eventually, if we are patient and courageous, we will discover the new direction in which God is leading us, and we will become involved with God in the new birthing process that is beginning within ourselves.

An example from my own experience may be helpful to demonstrate how fear may arise during imaginative prayer. I was going for a walk with Jesus along a quiet country road. I often went walking with him in my prayer time, and we usually ended up in a surprising situation. This was no exception. We came to a place where the landscape simply ended. Ahead of us was an imageless void, something like a white fog. I turned to look at Jesus but could not see him, though I sensed he was still nearby. I felt afraid, and unsure whether or not to continue into the unknown region ahead. I remembered a woman who had recently described to me a change in her prayer from being dominantly imaginative to becoming simply an experience of a void. She had been terrified for a time, but then had found it was simply a transition into a new way for her to experience God. My fear lessened as I recalled her experience. I looked toward the side of the road, and the woman was sitting there, looking toward me. She said nothing, but I had a sense of her being there to remind me that she had walked this way before me, and that it would be safe for me. I looked again for Jesus but still did not see him, though I still felt he was nearby and would be with me if I needed him. I gingerly and fearfully put out one foot, not knowing if there was any ground to step on. There was none, but I stepped out anyway, and found that I could walk in the void. I came at last to the edge of the fog-like atmosphere to a dark and limitless space where God seemed to be strongly present. Then I saw some beautifully colored abstract images of a kind I had not experienced before in prayer.

I know now that my fear had been a fear of the unknown and a natural resistance to a change in my relationship with God. I needed to stay with the fear and continue in the way Jesus was showing me, allowing him and the woman to strengthen me and encourage me. It was the beginning of a period of experiencing abstract images in my prayer which led me to discover a new dimension of God. My fear was both a sign of and a resistance to this new spiritual birth within my self.

We have considered two emotions that are often hidden from us in the shadow side of our inner child:

- anger, which calls for expression and then healing and forgiveness;
- fear, which calls for recognition and courage.

We will now look at a third area that is also commonly hidden in the shadow side of our inner child: sexuality. A small child is uninhibited in regard to sexuality. The genitals are as deserving of exploration and wonderment for the child as any other part of the world. As adults, most of us have learned to restrict our sexual exploration and activity to appropriate times and places. Hopefully, we also gained a sense of wonder and reverence toward our sexual organs in their potential for giving life and for expressing joyful and loving intimacy and pleasure.

Like some of our other feelings, we may have learned to repress our sexual feelings when we learned to restrict our sexual activity. We need to understand and believe that no emotions or feelings are right or wrong. Morality enters the picture only in our response to our emotions. Our feelings are morally neutral, neither good nor bad. Anger and sexual feelings seem to be the most likely of our feelings to be suppressed. This is mainly due to the strong cultural and religious moral codes concerning violence and sexual activity, and our failure to distinguish the activity from the emotion in regard to morality.

Psychotherapist Dr. M. Scott Peck discusses the strong resistance we have to dealing with both our anger and our sexual feelings: "The problem is not that human beings have such hostile and sexual feelings, but rather that human beings have a conscious mind that is so often unwilling to face these feelings and tolerate the pain of dealing with them, and that is so willing to sweep them under the rug" (*The Road Less Traveled,* Touchstone, Simon and Schuster, 1978). C. G. Jung coined the phrase, "The Wisdom of the Unconscious." It is this wonderful wisdom which we deny to our selves when we are unwilling to face and deal with these feelings and when, instead, we "sweep them under the rug" into our unconscious selves. We become deaf to the Wisdom of the Spirit whispering from deep within our selves, calling us to an ever fuller knowledge and love of our true selves and of our God revealed within our selves.

There seems to be a special spiritual gift in connection with our sexuality. Dr. Gerald May, a psychiatrist who is actively involved in the training of spiritual directors, describes this connection: "It has long been noted that the process of spiritual awakening and growth is associated with periods of rising sexual passion. In part this comes from the frank liberation of energy that accompanies lessening of attachments and release of psychological blocks. It is also connected with the awakening of ever deeper levels of love" (*Care of Mind/Care of Spirit,* Harper and Row, 1982). It is important that we not underestimate the power of cultural and religious sexual taboos to instill deep fear of the inner sexual experiences and images arising from our unconscious. We need to constantly and repeatedly distinguish our outer sexual activity from these inner sexual feelings, dreams, thoughts, and fantasies. This is one area in which we need to deliberately avoid one childlike characteristic: the tendency to identify fact with fantasy. We need to disconnect the outer taboos from our inner experience. Otherwise, we may turn away in fear and shame from some of the deepest and richest spiritual experiences because they are clothed in sexual garments. Sexual sensations and images can occur in prayer as powerfully moving expressions of our deep longing for God or of God's passion for us. We need to cultivate and revitalize our childlike sense of wonder and awe regarding sexuality. We need to allow our inner child to explore our sexual world, rejoicing in each discovery of the precious treasures hidden there.

Sexual imagery is one of the most eloquent expressions of our deep aching hunger for union with God and of our most intimate experiences of God. There is evidence of this in Scripture and in the writings of the mystics. For example, Teresa of Avila uses the image of marriage to express the experience of spiritual union with God (*The Interior Castle,* VII). The Song of Songs is an exquisitely poetic biblical portrayal of the mutual love between God as Lover and his people as the beloved. It describes, in the language of romantic love and courtship, God leading us to an exalted spiritual union with himself in a bond of love. Bernard of Clairvaux, a Christian mystic of the twelfth century, used the Song of Songs to describe the spiritual relationship between God and an individual.

Let us consider the male sexual image as a symbol for God as Lover. We may need to deliberately push aside our sexual taboos to free our selves to perceive him in this image—to let our inner child out to explore. Let us then look at what this male image could reveal to us about God.

Might this image tell us that God
　　is exceedingly full of life . . .
That he passionately desires
　　to be united with us in love . . .
That he longs to penetrate us deeply,

to the very center of our being . . .
That he yearns to implant the seed
 of divine life within us . . .
That our God is a passionate God
 who loves us deeply and
 who pursues us urgently and relentlessly?

Such imagery calls to mind Psalm 139:1–2, 7–10, 13–14:

O Lord, you have probed me and you know me:
 you know when I sit and when I stand;
 you understand my thoughts from afar.
Where can I go from your spirit?
 from your presence where can I flee?
If I go up to the heavens, you are there;
 if I sink to the nether world, you are present there.
If I take the wings of the dawn,
 if I settle at the farthest limits of the sea,
Even there your hand shall guide me,
 and your right hand hold me fast.
Truly you have formed my inmost being;
 you knit me in my mother's womb.
I give you thanks that I am fearfully, wonderfully made;
 wonderful are your works.

How sadly impoverished we might be in our experience of God if we were unable to experience his passionate love for us because of our inhibitions in regard to sexual fantasy. Let us be like little children, uninhibited and
open and receptive to the beautiful, life-giving sexual
images of God and of our relationship with him. Teresa of
Avila writes with childlike simplicity, and she reveals her
passion for God at every turn. One image which is sugges-
tive of sexual penetration is the "wound of love." She
describes this experience in *The Interior Castle,* VI: "It
seems this pain reaches to the soul's very depths and that
when He who wounds it draws out the arrow, it indeed

seems, in accord with the deep love the soul feels, that God is drawing these very depths after Him. . . . This delightful pain—and it is not pain—is not continuous, although sometimes it lasts a long while; at other times it goes away quickly." Teresa eagerly invites us to follow her in her passionate journey to God: "How important it is for you not to impede your Spouse's celebration of this spiritual marriage with your souls, since this marriage brings so many blessings, as you will see" (*The Interior Castle,* VII). Let us not become trapped in a false humility by listening to that little voice within that might be saying, "Who am I to think I could be as close to God as Teresa of Avila?" Let us remember our angelic capacity portrayed in the nativity scene and embrace the mystic within our selves. Let us be passionate in our pursuit of God and let us desire his passionate penetration of us to the depths of our being!

So far, we have considered only the masculine side of God. It is very natural for Christians to view God as masculine. Jesus presents God to us as Father; Church tradition and Scripture (as in the Song of Songs) present God as Lover and his people as bride. Most of us have grown up with these masculine images of God. It is good to remember that all of our images or concepts of God are limited. Humanly speaking, we are simply unable to imagine an infinite God; we cannot confine God to the limited capacity of our minds. Recognizing this, we would do well to be open to a variety of images of God, and to be constantly ready and willing to expand our present notions of God.

Having considered the male sexual image of God, let us now look to the complementary female sexual image and see what it might reveal to us of the feminine side of God. Again, we may need to deliberately and with some effort set aside our sexual taboos, so that we can see the image with our vision uninhibited by these restricting blinders—letting our adventurous inner child explore with eager curiosity and wonder. What, then, can this female sexual symbol for God reveal to us about her?

Might this image tell us that God is open and receptive,
    passionately desiring us to enter deeply within
    her . . .
Yearning for us to penetrate her so deeply that
    we become engulfed in her tender embrace . . .
So deeply, indeed, that we might enter
    completely within her
    and become lost in the depths of her womb . . .
Become like an unborn child
    united with her, one with her,
    receiving divine life from her . . .
Then in time . . . brought to birth again
    and delivered from the womb of God . . .
    to share our divine life with others?

Can we say that God is like that for us? Can we allow the desire to arise within our selves to penetrate God and be lost in her, become one with her? If we can accept and embrace our sexual inner child in shadow, that child may indeed come into the light and become a precious treasure in our life with God—freely, passionately, intensely living and loving life as the precious child of our passionate God.

Kahlil Gibran expresses beautifully the integration of this passionate child in a balanced manner within our selves, as he speaks of Reason and Passion in *The Prophet* (Alfred A. Knopf, Inc., 1923, 1951):

Your soul is oftentimes a battlefield, upon which your reason and your judgment wage war against your passion and your appetite.

Would that I could be the peacemaker in your soul, that I might turn the discord and the rivalry of your elements into oneness and melody.

But how shall I, unless you yourselves be also the peacemakers, nay, the lovers of all your elements?

Your reason and your passion are the rudder and the sails of your seafaring soul.

If either your sails or your rudder be broken, you can but toss and drift, or else be held at a standstill in mid-seas.

For reason, ruling alone, is a force confining; and passion, unattended, is a flame that burns to its own destruction.

Therefore let your soul exalt your reason to the height of passion, that it may sing;

And let it direct your passion with reason, that your passion may live through its own daily resurrection, and like the phoenix rise above its own ashes. . . .

Among the hills, when you sit in the cool shade of the white poplars, sharing the peace and serenity of distant fields and meadows—then let your heart say in silence, "God rests in reason."

And when the storm comes, and the mighty wind shakes the forest, and thunder and lightning proclaim the majesty of the sky,—then let your heart say in awe, "God moves in passion."

And since you are a breath in God's sphere, and a leaf in God's forest, you too should rest in reason and move in passion.

One particular aspect of our inner sexual child which we often find difficult to accept concerns sexual fantasies. Such fantasies are likely to occur with increased frequency and intensity during a period of rising sexual passion which, as Gerald May has pointed out, may be associated with a time of spiritual awakening. There are three areas which can be sources of needless worry and guilt over such sexual fantasies; they can be real barriers to the process of spiritual awakening and growth. The first area is that of the sexual moral code which governs our outer sexual conduct, but which we may mistakenly apply to our inner sexual fantasies. Fantasies, like emotions, are neither good nor bad but morally neutral. Also like our feelings, fantasies can be valuable signs from our unconscious depths—whisperings of the Spirit within.

The second source of worry over sexual fantasies is the fear that we will act out our fantasy in our external life. As a matter of fact, the opposite is true. Sexual fantasies are similar to violent fantasies in this regard. If we act out in violent fantasy our feelings of anger and desire for revenge, we are much less likely to act them out in our external life. If we act out in fantasy our sexual feelings and desires, we are also much less likely to act them out in fact. Having given our passion recognition and expression in fantasy, we are much better able to direct our passion with reason.

The third source of worry regarding sexual fantasies concerns the person who is involved in our fantasies. As spiritual pilgrims in need of guidance and companionship on our journey, many of us are likely to have entered into spiritual direction. As a normal and natural accompaniment to such an intimate relationship, we probably experience feelings of warmth and affection toward our spiritual director or guide. If our spiritual guide is a person of the opposite sex, she or he is likely to be involved in our sexual fantasies. This is especially likely to occur at the outset of this period of rising energy. We find our selves suddenly infused with passion and it is not at all easy to immediately identify God as the true object of our feelings. A human person is a much more natural player in our sexual fantasies, especially a person with whom we have already formed a warm and intimate relationship. When this occurs, we may well experience feelings of confusion, guilt, fear, and shame. These feelings can arise from one or both of the first two sources we have just discussed, as well as from a perception that sexuality and spirituality are not related. We may think that sexuality has no place at all in spiritual direction—that it is not a fit topic of concern or discussion. Nothing could be farther from the truth. We are essentially, at the core of our being, in the depth of our soul, sexual beings. If we exclude the sexual dimensions of our selves from our spiritual direction process, we seriously reduce the effectiveness of that process in nurturing our spiritual growth. In effect, we leave our inner sexual child outside the door when we enter the room for our meeting with our spiritual guide, and that is very sad. Our child sits outside on the doorstep, rejected and lonely, crying in sorrow—while we sit inside wondering why we feel not quite like our true self, not fully at ease, inhibited in our conversation with our spiritual director.

How can we deal with our sexual fantasies in ways that may help to allay our confusion and shame and fear—so that we can celebrate this graced spiritual awakening rather than deny or suppress it? First of all, we may need to summon up our courage and debate with our selves on our preconceived notions about our sexual taboos in fact and fantasy. Second, we may need to take a new look at our attitude toward fantasy and our possible fear of acting out our fantasies in our external behavior. We need to revive our inner child, who delights in fantasy of all kinds; we need to learn to enjoy fantasy again, the way we did when we were children. Third, if we find a disturbance or inhibition in our relationship with our spiritual guide, we need to talk it over with him or her. It may take a great deal of courage to broach the subject. We will need to bring our inner child in with us and, probably feeling childlike or childish, tell our director the story of what is going on, including our feelings of confusion and shame and fear. Then we can involve our whole selves in the spiritual direction process, thereby freeing the process to be as spiritually nourishing as it is intended to be.

We can encourage the integration of our sexuality into our spiritual journey during our prayer time by deliberately introducing sexual imagery and letting our imagination go free to explore as a child—curious, adventurous, and uninhibited by outer taboos. The Song of Songs would be an excellent scriptural passage to use. We could also imagine conversations and activities with Jesus, Mary, Joseph, or other biblical figures, or favorite saints, and allow warm, romantic and affectionate feelings to enter into those relationships as they develop. This prayer activity can help to direct our great loving energy and desire toward its proper object: God—incarnated and revealed to us through those spiritual figures to whom we are attracted.

A personal prayer experience of mine might help to illustrate the value and role of our inner shadow child in our spiritual journey. This occurred after several months of recognizing and dealing with anger that I had suppressed for some time. In my prayer, Jesus stood before me with his hand out, wanting me to go with him. He seemed to need me for something. I took his hand and began to walk with him. We began walking down some steep, circular stairs. It felt very precarious, and I held on to Jesus tightly to keep from falling. At the bottom, there were dark tunnels through which we walked, coming finally to a black prison cell. Jesus needed my help to open it, and so together we turned the key and unlocked the door. Jesus waited outside. It seemed he could do no more, and it was up to me to free the prisoner within. I entered the cell and found the prisoner to be a small, coal-black creature the size of a tiny infant curled up in the corner in a fetal position. It was very ugly and had long black claws. I could not possibly imagine a more hideous-looking creature. Strangely, I felt no revulsion or fear, but was only intent on freeing it. I sat down near the creature and said, "I love you." It became upset, and said it was unlovable and selfish and hateful. I said, "I still love you. I'm like that too, sometimes, and Jesus loves me and loves you, too." The creature did not believe me. It curled up into an even tighter ball. I reached out, gently picked it up and cuddled it in my lap, repeating, "I love you." Finally, still getting no response, I cupped its chin in my hand and raised its face to look at me as I looked back at it with gentleness and love. The creature's face was transformed. It looked like my granddaughter, Michelle, who was two years old at the time. Then her entire body was transformed and she stood beside me, a beautiful child in a pretty party dress. She said she wasn't sure if she liked being a child. I told her I thought it was a wonderful way to be. I took her outside the prison cell to Jesus, who was still waiting outside. He swept her into his arms and hugged her and wept for joy. I found my self crying also, at the sight of such a happy reunion. I could see how very special this child was to Jesus, and the deep joy he felt when she was set free and back in his arms.

This experience spoke eloquently to me about the role of my own inner child in shadow. Much of what it said to me is true for all of us as we seek to discover, to accept and to embrace our inner child. First of all, Jesus leads us to our imprisoned child—the part of our inner child we deny and repress because we do not want to admit we have this or that childish tendency in us. We do not want to see it. We do not want it in the light. We imprison it in darkness deep within our selves.

We cannot consciously seek out and bring to light our shadow, for by its very definition, the shadow is in our unconscious and we are therefore unaware of its existence. We can discover it only by listening to the clues and messages arising from our unconscious self—the whispering of the Spirit of the Lord from deep within our selves. In the case of this experience of mine, it arose in meditation and was a surprise throughout. The surprising, spontaneous element is a good clue with which to identify an imaginary experience as one that is arising from our unconscious depths.

Not only did Jesus lead the way, but it was steep and frightening. I could not have navigated those steep stairs without Jesus to hold on to, to help me keep my balance and avoid falling into the depths and possibly incurring a serious injury. Though the way down to the unconscious is indeed frightening, Jesus will always be with us to guide and protect us. He has promised he will be with us always and he keeps his promises. We need but to call on him when we are frightened, to reach out for his hand when we feel endangered.

Though Jesus had the key to the prison cell, he could not open it by himself. We had to do it together. Then I had to enter and free my shadow child by my self, though Jesus remained close by outside. I could feel his support and encouragement, but I had to do this by my self. The Lord cannot make our choices for us. He leaves us free, but he will be with us.

Because of its sheer blackness, hideous looks and ferocious claws, I recognized the small imprisoned creature to be my own shadow. Even though we bring to light and deal with our shadow, the destructive tendencies remain. We all have within our selves the potential for the most hideous evil imaginable. The task is to recognize it, accept it, and bring it to light so that we can consciously direct it.

The fact that I could truly love this ugly little creature and embrace it was surprising. It showed me that even though I could acknowledge and embrace my hostile tendencies as a part of my self they would always seem dark and ugly to me, and appropriately so. It was in and through my loving and embracing that my shadow self was transformed to an "adorable little angel" of a child. This is, in fact, the result of our total acceptance of our selves: the freeing of our hidden goodness—the angelic, the adorable, the Divine Child within. As Jesus said, "Whoever welcomes one such child for my sake welcomes me" (Matthew 18:5).

Jung has said that our shadow is ninety percent pure gold. Hidden behind each of our shadows there lies a corresponding dormant goodness in need of freeing. It is a major task of the spiritual journey to repeatedly uncover and learn to live with our various shadow tendencies at ever deeper and more subtle levels, thereby freeing more and more of our innate goodness, our godliness. Each shadow characteristic has its corresponding goodness and light. For example, accepting and directing our hostile tendencies frees our just anger to energize us to take action to right injustices and oppressions of our selves and others; or getting in touch with our arrogance and pride frees a deeper humility.

Just as the characteristics of the child in light have the common quality of simplicity or humility, the characteristics of the child in shadow have an opposite underlying characteristic: *pride*. It is our pride that causes us to resist becoming small and helpless and childlike before God. Pride underlies our desire to be in control and to form our selves into the shape we think we should be, rather than allowing God to shape us in God's own image in ways we cannot see. We need to acknowledge and embrace our prideful, arrogant, stubborn child in order to free our humble, simple child to come to light and run into God's open and welcoming arms.

It is significant that my shadow image took the form of a little child. Most of the characteristics which we find difficult to acknowledge in our selves were planted there in our childhood. They are taken on as a part of our normal growth as our parents, church leaders, and others in authority told us, in words or by actions or implications, the things we should or should not do. It is as though we each have an inner tape recorder. We operate the controls and are responsible for what we record, play back, and erase. As children we had not learned to discriminate among the various messages given us by others. We just pushed the "record" button and let it run all the time. We all have a special tape in our inner collection on which we recorded all the "shoulds" and "should nots" of those whom we perceived as authority figures. We need to teach our inner child how to edit this tape. It is a major task of our spiritual journey to look at each "should" or "should not" in turn and translate it to a free choice. We need to show our child how to listen to an old message and record a new message over it, erasing the old one in the process. For example, we may have a message that says, "It is cowardly to feel afraid." We can record over it a new message that says, "It is human to feel afraid. It may be cowardly to run away and it may also be wise to run away. It is courageous to act in spite of fear." It can be helpful to write out both old and new messages; it can strengthen and reinforce the editing to actually record it physically. Then we can show our inner child how to play the new message repeatedly until it becomes a part of our selves. We can then be free to acknowledge our fear and make more responsible decisions about how we will respond to it.

As we go through the process with our child of editing the tape, we will make an interesting discovery. As each message is edited and the "shoulds" and "should nots" are deleted, we acquire a keener ear. We are able to hear increasingly subtle authority messages that we are surprised were there. The editing process may in fact be lifelong. Not only are there old messages that are difficult to hear, but our inner child seems to like to record new authority messages when we are not supervising. We need to keep up our vigilance and continue our search for the hidden messages our child records.

We can be guided in our search by our inner wisdom, the Spirit of the Lord deep within. We can become ever more adept at perceiving the signals which surface from deep within our selves and point the way to an inner shadow child lost or imprisoned by an inappropriate authority message.

Let us search unceasingly for our little lost children imprisoned or wandering within our selves, calling them home to us and embracing them with total and passionate love. Let us welcome into our arms our whole child, both dark and light sides. Let us open wide our hearts and sweep our adorable, divine child into our arms, reunited with us in a total and unconditional act of love, the same kind of love our God lavishes upon each one of us.

5

Nurturing the Child

We have given considerable attention to the characteristics and role of our inner child in the spiritual journey. We have also considered some of the supporting characters in the drama of our journey—those aspects of our selves that are portrayed in the nativity scene and that play an important part in bringing to birth and nurturing the Divine Child within our selves as this birthing process occurs repeatedly along our journey.

Now let us look with more attention at the nurturing aspect of our spiritual growth, at those characteristics that tend to encourage the healthy growth of our newborn divine life. Parents—mother and father—are the primary providers of such nurturing. We have ample imagery for spiritual fathering. One is the obvious image of God as Father, described by Jesus. Another is the father-image of Joseph. The fathering characteristics of Joseph as seen in the nativity story would be worthwhile to return to occasionally and to ponder in an attempt to enlarge and deepen our image of God as Father. All of us, women as well as men, need to incorporate ever more fully our own inner father, both to nurture our child within and to allow the image of God to shine forth from us ever more visibly.

We will turn now to look more closely at spiritual mothering. All of us, men as well as women, also need to develop our own inner mother to balance the parenting of our child and to allow a fuller image of God to become visible through us—an image which incorporates the feminine side of God.

Jesus has provided us with an image and model of mothering in his own mother, Mary. The feminine side of God is made visible in her. This gift of Jesus to us is symbolically highlighted in the scene of the crucifixion as described in John's Gospel:

> Seeing his mother there with the disciple whom he loved, Jesus said to his mother, "Woman, there is your son." In turn he said to the disciple, "There is your mother" (John 19:26–27).

We have explored in some depth the image of Mary as revealed in the conception and birth of Jesus. Let us expand and deepen the image further by looking at Mary as she is portrayed in other Scripture stories.

Both Matthew's and Luke's Gospels refer to Mary as "virgin." We have tended to limit our understanding of Mary's virginity to the physical level of meaning. It can be greatly enriched and deeply significant for our own spiritual journey if we expand our concept of virginity and look at its inner, spiritual significance. "Virgin" in the ancient symbolic sense of the word meant "she who is one-in-herself." We need to find our selves consciously as one-in-ourself, separate from the various roles we play in our lives. Only when we find our selves to some degree as one-in-ourself can we find the true relationships and meanings within our various roles. We will look at Mary in the scriptural stories from the point of view of her virginity, her becoming one-in-herself.

Early in Luke's Gospel, we find Mary "pondering in her heart," reflecting on events that are mysterious. The first instance occurs after the birth of Jesus and the visit of the shepherds (Luke 2:19). Just as she waited for the coming-to-term of her infant, so she is now willing to wait for the meaning of the mystery to be unveiled to her in time. She does not need to know the answers immediately, but can wait and watch, pondering them in her heart as opposed to analyzing them in her head.

The second instance of Mary's pondering takes place when Jesus is twelve years old, becomes separated from Mary and Joseph after the Passover celebration in Jerusalem, and is found by them in the temple in a discussion with the teachers (Luke 2:41–52). When questioned by them, Jesus says to Mary and Joseph, "Why did you search for me? Did you not know I had to be in my Father's house?" Jesus' parents are astonished and confused. Again, Mary waits and ponders, holding the mystery in her heart, willing to allow it to unfold in time.

This willingness of Mary to wait and to watch, to allow mystery to reveal itself to her while she simply pays attention to the rhythms and movements of her heart, is the main characteristic of contemplation. Mary is truly a model for contemplation, and in this sense a model of true Christian discipleship. She exemplifies for us an essential mark of the disciple, which is to follow the call to contemplation—the call of the Lord to listen ever more attentively to the voice of the Spirit within. Only then are we able to follow the true way of the Lord in our external actions, guided from within by the Spirit of God.

In these two early events in the life of Jesus, Mary gives an impression of a woman who is open to life, presently confused by the mystery which enters it, but willing to live with the confusion for a time. She is becoming progressively more whole, more focused and centered within her self. She is becoming one-in-herself.

Mary's growth in this spiritual process is demonstrated in a remarkable way at her next appearance in the Gospels, at the wedding feast of Cana (John 2:1–10). During the feast, the wine runs out and Mary says to Jesus, "They have no more wine." Jesus replies to her, "Woman, how does this concern of yours involve me? My hour has not yet come." Saying no more to Jesus, Mary turns to the waiters and says, "Do whatever he tells you." This is quite a change from the young woman who was confused, somewhat unsure of her self, and unable to understand her twelve-year-old son. In contrast, Mary now is extremely self-assured and confident that she knows her son and his characteristic behavior and attitudes. She must know that he is flexible and can change his plans. She also must know that he highly values her perceptions. She is confident in the relationship that has developed between them as they both matured over the years. It is noteworthy that Jesus addresses her as "woman" rather than "mother," signifying more of a partnership or friendship rather than a parent-child relationship. Mary is so secure in her relationship with Jesus that she does not even reply to his objections. She simply expects him to value her clear and compassionate view of the situation and respond. This is quite a strong woman! She certainly is one-in-herself. She has become truly virgin.

The inner strength displayed by Mary is characteristic of having grown to this unity within her self. She knows her self well and accepts her whole self. She has found a good and true relationship with her own masculine side, shown in her ability to take decisive and assertive action. It is a "happy marriage" with her feminine sensitivity and compassion.

Mary's inner wholeness, her close union with the Spirit of God within her self, now enables her to extend God's love to more and more people externally. Such is the depth of her union with God that she is able to become mother to the entire human race. This gift was symbolically expressed by Jesus from the cross, in the passage from John's Gospel previously discussed. Jesus presented Mary as mother to "the disciple whom he loved" or, in other words, to each one of us. Again we notice

Jesus addressing Mary as "woman," a repeated affirmation of her inner wholeness.

Mary is the image of our Mothering God. As she extends her arms to us in compassion and tenderness, we see God reaching her arms out to her children. She wants to embrace us all and nurse us with her warm, sweet milk that we may grow strong and wise and good. She feels a painful urgency when we do not or cannot accept her loving care, as a mother whose breasts are painfully full with pressure from the stored milk that cannot flow. She seeks us out, beseeching us to come into her open arms, to be nourished at her breasts and to be filled with her abundant life.

We can encourage the development of our own femininity or of our feminine side, and at the same time experience more fully the feminine side of God, by deliberately spending time with Mary during our prayer time. We can imagine any of the Scripture stories in which she is involved. It is important to be aware of our feelings toward her and of our impressions of her feelings and attitudes toward us. One story which is potentially very powerful is the wedding feast of Cana. For example, we might imagine our selves to be Mary, or to stand beside her as she tells Jesus that the wine has run out. Listen to his reply very attentively, being aware of your own feelings and reactions and your impressions of his attitude toward Mary and your self. An older translation of Jesus' reply, "What would you have me do, woman?" may be more effective than the more modern ones in this particular conversation with Mary (John 2:4, Confraternity Edition).

As we encourage the development of our image of God as Mother or Father, it is important to be aware of a common barrier that blocks the way for most of us at one time or another. This barrier is our limited image of parents that was formed through our childhood relationships with our human mother and father, or those who took their place in our formative years. No human parent can love a child with the constant and totally unconditional love with which God loves each of us. And yet our image of God as parent depends for its formation upon that limited image from our childhood. Without that image, we would have no concept at all of what a parent is like, and therefore of what God is like as a parent.

It is as though we look at God through a pair of eyeglasses, one lens formed from a prescription determined by our mother and the other by our father. We literally can focus on God only through these lenses. As we grow, our experience expands to include other parent figures. We discover God-like qualities in other adults which we did not find in our parents, and we outgrow our present prescription. We replace the old lenses with new ones through which we can see God a little more clearly, with our vision expanded.

Sometimes one or both of the lenses are cracked or shattered, and we either cannot find God at all or God seems very distant and out of focus or distorted. When we are able to see with only one eye we lose our depth perception. God may seem "flat." At such a time, we may feel emotionally distant from God. Our prayer may seem dry. Our image of God is broken by our memory of a parent or parent figure in an experience which shattered our trust in him or her. We may have felt abandoned, betrayed, misunderstood, unloved. It does not matter whether or not our parent intended to hurt us. What matters is our perception of the experience. We literally see God through the lens of that experience and we are afraid to trust God, afraid of further abandonment or betrayal or hurt. The shattered lens needs to be replaced. The memory needs to be healed in order to see God more clearly and to believe in and accept God's love.

In order to form a new lens to replace the broken one, we need to look at the shattering experience again, from our present viewpoint. We need to relive it, but in a new way. One very effective way to do this is to imagine our self back in the situation. The difference is that this time we can do and say in our imagination what we could not do or say as a child. We can also bring with us a supportive person—perhaps Jesus or Mary. Depending on the depth of our wound, we are likely to experience the surfacing of more or less intense emotions that may have lain dormant for years. It is important to allow these feelings to emerge and to experience their full intensity. We can do or say in our imagination whatever we feel like doing or saying. We can scream and rage, sob in pain, tell our parent how we feel in the midst of our tears, throw a tantrum or inflict a punishment—until our feelings are spent for the moment. We may want to speak more calmly to our parent then, and perhaps imagine his or her response. Or we may wish to leave at that point, perhaps to continue later.

It can be very helpful to write out a dialogue with our parent before or after this imaginative experience. It can help us to get in touch with our feelings from a different perspective. As the dialogue progresses, we often find that it begins to flow more spontaneously, and we may find ourselves writing surprising questions or responses, gaining a clearer insight of the situation or triggering an unexpected emotional response. It is important not to rationalize our way out of our feelings with such thoughts as, "Now I understand why he/she did that, so I should not feel hurt or angry anymore." Our feelings will run their course in time, but not if we deny them at this point. We can end up covering with a bandaid a wound that has a deeper infection and needs a longer time to heal.

We can also write a letter to our parent expressing our feelings and thoughts. The letter or the written dialogue or the imaginative experience is not intended to be shared with our parent. Such are simply ways for us to get in touch with the experience and to bring it to resolution and healing within our selves. It could be destructive to share it at this point. We may or may not choose to write or talk with our parent later.

If the memory we are dealing with was deeply painful, it may take a relatively long time to come to healing and forgiveness. It is important not to hurry the process. We may need to mourn the death of what we had hoped for in our relationship with our parent. We may experience all the stages of grieving: denial, anger, bargaining, depression and acceptance. The stages are likely to overlap; they are not likely to occur neatly in that order.

When the healing process has been allowed to come to completion in time, we can recognize it by the gift of the ability to forgive our parent. This does not mean that we will no longer feel hurt or angry or guilty in remembering the experience. It also does not mean that the experience will not surface from our memory at a later time and need further healing. Sometimes a hurt that seems to be healed recurs later and needs to be dealt with at a deeper level or in a different aspect. Forgiveness does mean that we are able to accept our parents as they are, with all their human limitations. It means that we are able to let go of the way we wanted and perhaps still want our parents to love us; we are able to accept the limited way in which they do love us.

In this process of letting go, we let the shattered lens of our painful experience fall from our eye glasses. We allow it to be replaced with a new lens through which we can see God offering us the kind of unlimited love we deeply desire, but which no human parents can give us. Then, childlike, we can run into the open arms of our God and receive the totally unconditional love that only God can give. We can feel deeply the strong, protective arms of God our Father, the soft, tender embrace of God our Mother.

Let us now consider some of the other ways our nurturing God is revealed to us. A child is nurtured not only by parents but through brothers and sisters, members of the extended family, and friends. The child's growth is greatly enriched by this variety of relationships. Like a child, we can enhance our spiritual journey by seeking to develop spiritual relationships with others who can show us God's love and care and wisdom, each in her or his own unique and special way. With childlike openness, we can reach out in our prayer time and invite others to spend time with us. For example, we might ask a favorite saint or biblical figure to join us. You may be surprised to find that if you invite and encourage a few such relationships, your circle of spiritual friends and guides will soon expand. The result may be a wonderful enrichment of your experience of God and a revitalizing of your prayer.

Such has been my own experience, which I will share with you in hopes that you may be encouraged to welcome others into your own spiritual journey. I had a circle of spiritual friends and guides who appeared regularly and sat with me each time I prayed for about a year. It began one day when I felt upset and frightened as I sat down to pray. I was aware of Jesus sitting very close to me on my left and Mary on my right. They both had their arms around me in love and support. After a few moments, I noticed Francis of Assisi and Ignatius of Loyola next to Jesus, and Therese of Lisieux (the "Little Flower") and my daughter Kathy next to Mary. They formed a tight circle, and I felt tremendous strength and love from them. Before this time, I had regularly spent time with Jesus through imaginary participation in the Gospel stories with him. He had grown more and more personal to me, and I felt him to be a close friend and guide on my journey, always there when I needed him and often challenging me and encouraging me to new frontiers.

Occasionally my daughter Kathy had shown up in my prayer-imagery, and usually Jesus and Mary were with her. Once or twice, Therese was with Kathy; she had become a favorite of Kathy's through some stories about the "Little Flower" that I had read often to her. Francis and Ignatius appeared spontaneously one time when I had continued a dream in active imagination during my prayer time. Both had become significant to me through association with some very special Franciscan friars and Jesuit priests.

During Advent, a week or so after the "prayer circle" had first begun, I thought about Joseph and invited him to join us, which he did willingly. After that, Teresa of Avila asked to join the circle. It took me a little while to recognize her and what she was asking, but when I finally did, she also became a part of my wonderful group of spiritual friends. Later, after praying with a Scripture story involving Peter, he seemed to want to stay and join us, so I welcomed him also into the circle. Some time later, I decided I would like to have my spiritual director in the circle to pray with me, and so I imagined him to be there. This led to the most unusual member of my prayer circle joining a few days later—his collie, Megan, who had died shortly before that time. She was a very significant figure in my spiritual experience. Analogous to the sheep of the nativity story, Megan helped and challenged me to be in touch with my "animal instincts," my sensuality and sexuality and my emotions in general. My spiritual director did not play an active role in my prayer experiences. He was simply a part of the circle, supportive but silent. This seemed natural and appropriate to me, for my dialogue with him was conducted externally.

From the first day on, my prayer circle was there with me each time I prayed, for about a year. They supported and encouraged me, they loved and challenged me, each in his or her special way. Similar to an extended family, my relationship with each one is unique. Peter is like a brother. Therese of Lisieux is like a sister to Kathy and like a grown daughter to me. Joseph is father and friend. Teresa of Avila and Francis are friends and companions. Ignatius is like a spiritual director. Mary is mother, with my self sometimes as a little child and sometimes as a grown daughter. Jesus remains the dominant figure in my prayer as always, with his role varying as friend, lover, guide— the Lord of my prayer journey.

After about a year it seemed to be time to leave the security of this "family circle" and explore new ways of prayer, much like a daughter leaving for college. I went through a period of homesickness, mourning their seeming loss, missing the security of their constant presence. I know now that this change was necessary for the development of my prayer, for I began to discover new ways of spending my time with God, exploring new territory on my journey. I have also discovered that my spiritual family and friends still care deeply and will come to be with me whenever I want or need one of them.

My prayer circle was and is a precious gift to me. It continues to be a mystery to me, beyond my comprehension. I know not why they came, for I certainly did not do anything to deserve such a gift, and it never occurred to me to ask for it. I surely welcomed their coming and was often overcome with gratitude and joy over their presence. My inner child came to birth many times in their midst. I have danced for joy, sobbed in sorrow or fear, sung with them in praise, raged in anger, resisted and then accepted their challenges—all in the sure and unshakable knowledge of their unconditional love for me. They constantly show me the many faces of God's unbelievably great love for me and for all of us.

I am convinced that we all have special spiritual friends and family who would like to accompany and guide us on our journey—those who have gone before us through death into the spiritual realm, whether they are officially recognized saints or others we have known. Perhaps they are only waiting for an invitation, or a sign that they would be welcome. Perhaps we need only to believe in them—to believe that they are near, that they care deeply, and that they will be with us if we want them. Perhaps they eagerly desire to come to us, to assist at the births of our inner children, and to nurse and nurture us to strength and wholeness.

It is important to realize that each of us is unique in the way we experience spiritual reality. Obviously, visual imagery is a dominant way for me. However, not only are images themselves distinctly different for each of us, but the kind of imagery varies. It can include not only visual images but sound, touch, smell, or taste. Besides images, we may sense a certain feeling or mood, or simply recognize the presence of God or another spiritual being. The point of sharing the experience of my prayer circle is to encourage you to be open and receptive to new experiences, and to remove or overcome barriers and resistances as they occur. One barrier could be the expectation that if any saints were to join you, they would be perceived through a visual image such as I experienced. That expectation could result in failing to accept or simply missing completely an experience that may be manifest in a different way, such as in a simple sense of presence. Another barrier could be a false humility in which we feel unworthy of the attention of such great saints. This is a failure to accept our inner angel, our mystical nature, our call from the Lord to draw ever closer. Let us not clip the wings of our angels through such false humility. Rather, let us willingly allow our selves to be lifted to the heights to which we are called by God.

It is also important to realize that our spiritual experiences are gifts from God. We cannot determine the time nor the place nor the manner in which they are given. All we can do is to be available to receive them. We can set aside a regular time for prayer; we can cultivate an open, receptive attitude and attempt to remove barriers and resistances as we discover them. We can also ask God for whatever we want. Our deep desire for a closer union with God was implanted within us by the Spirit. It is certainly good to express our desires to God as a little child standing before a loving parent. Like any good parent, God will answer our plea in the way and at the time that is best for us, and probably differently from what we expect—for

God does enjoy lavishing us with surprise gifts, and knows how we as little children delight in receiving them. If spiritual friends and family come to join us on our journey, it is a gift from God. Let us keep our arms open and ready to receive this precious gift.

Let us reach out with our child's hands
    and invite all those who are dear to us . . .
        welcoming them into the circle
        of our family . . .
    welcome them as our mothers and fathers . . .
        our sisters and brothers . . .
        our sons and daughters . . .
        aunts and uncles and cousins . . .
        grandmothers and grandfathers . . .
        human friends and animal friends . . .
        lovers and beloved.
Let us bask in their love . . .
    draw from their strength . . .
        rise to their challenges.
Let us be born and die
    in their arms . . .
        laugh and cry . . .
            rant and rave . . .
                dance and sing . . .
    in fear and courage . . .
        in sorrow and in pain . . .
            in faith and hope and love . . .
                in praise and in thanksgiving.
Let us look upon their faces
    and see the face of God . . .
let us listen to their words
    and hear the voice of God . . .
let us touch their hands
    and feel the hand of God . . .
let us run into their arms
    and be lost in God's embrace.

6

The Child— Dying and Rising

We come full circle over and over again in our spiritual journey toward union with God. Our circle does not bring us back to the original starting point, however, but to a new point beyond the place where we began. It is a spiral effect.

This spiraling path toward wholeness begins with the conception of new life deep within our selves. There is a coming to birth, and a time of nurturing and growth. There is a dying—a letting go of the old to make way for the new. There follows a resurrection to new life, and the cycle begins anew. The Divine Child is born, grows, dies and rises to new life over and over again.

Often the death is a painful and violent one. Sometimes we are brought face to face with our unspeakably hideous shadow child. We see the darkest part of our selves and we cannot stand it, so we mercilessly crucify our shadow child. When we repent and accept forgiveness from God and from our selves, we allow the body of our dead shadow child to be taken down from the cross, laid into our mothering arms and embraced. It is the turning point on the circle. It is the moment of reconciliation and inner unity—the moment when resurrection becomes possible. When we accept God's love and forgiveness of our darkest selves, we let go of our own notion of who we should be, and we accept God's view of who we are. We turn around. We are reconciled with our inner child. Then the goodness and beauty of the child are revealed in the light of God's vision, and new life is released. The new life brings to us an increased clarity of vision and sharpness of hearing. We are able to detect deeper, subtler stirrings of the Spirit within our selves. A new cycle can begin.

In his poignantly beautiful sculpture, the Pieta, Michelangelo has given us a model for the turning point on our circular path, the moment of forgiveness and reconciliation. Mary holds in her arms the crucified body of her child. Put to death like a common criminal, crucified between two thieves, branded as a traitor, Jesus now rests in his mother's arms. She embraces him in love, seeing his goodness in the light of God's vision—seeing him as her Divine Child.

Let us explore the Pieta in a contemplative prayer experience. Let us take a long and loving look at this powerful image, paying attention to the stirrings of our hearts. Begin by looking slowly and attentively at the photographs of the Pieta on the following pages. Linger often as you go, savoring the images and becoming aware of your emotions as they surface.

Pay special attention to Mary. Notice her face. She looks very young. It is certainly not the face of a woman in her forties, which would be her physical age at the time of Jesus' death. Perhaps Michelangelo has portrayed her inner disposition, her memory of holding the infant Jesus in her arms as a young mother. Her right arm reinforces this maternal impression, as she holds him cradled. She even has her robe wrapped around him, like a baby wrapped in a blanket. The fullness of her breasts portrays nurturing . . . softness . . . cradling . . . comforting. As she received him into her arms at birth, she receives him again at death. Returning to her face, we can see the depth of her sorrow and compassion, paradoxically coupled with a deep peace and serenity.

Mary's right hand and arm express strength . . . power . . . endurance . . . as well as receptivity. Her feet and legs reveal a corresponding sense of stability and security. Her left hand suggests another memory, the event of Jesus' conception in her womb—the annunciation. It brings to mind her reply to the angel, "I am the servant of the Lord. Let it be done to me as you say" (Luke 1:38). Just as she surrendered to God's will at Jesus' conception, so her hand seems to declare again her surrender to God and her total acceptance of Jesus' death, even in the midst of the deep pain and loss she experiences. Mary's entire body suggests openness, receptivity and acceptance.

Take time to look at Mary as deeply as possible. Search carefully for the emotions and dispositions revealed to you. Let your impressions soak in.

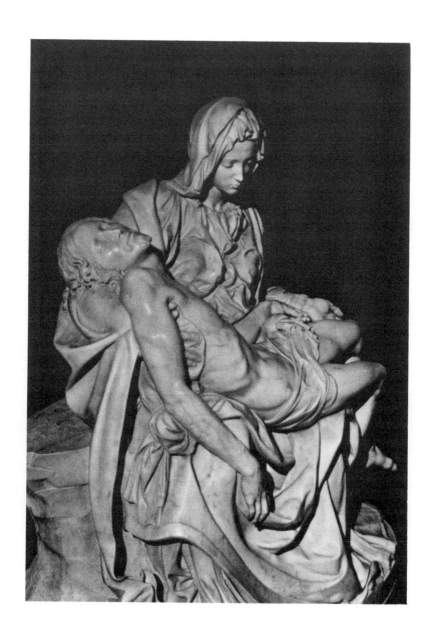

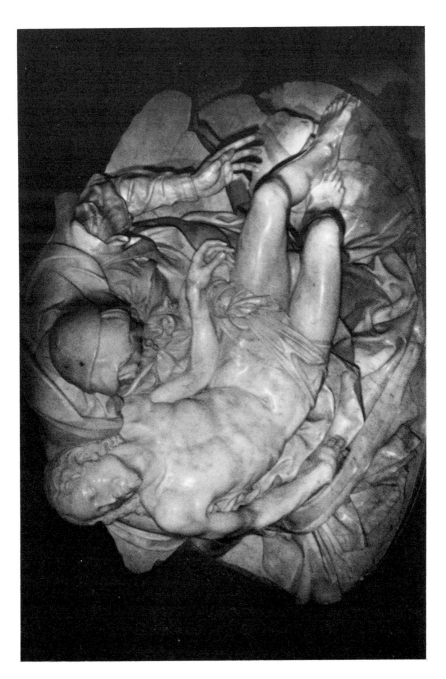

Now I encourage you to get in touch with your own inner Mary. Take on the feelings and dispositions you perceive in the sculpture. Assume the same position as Mary. Be Mary. Sit with your feet planted firmly on the ground like hers. Extend your arms and hands in the same position as hers. Tilt your head at the same angle and try to take on her facial expression.

Now focus your attention on the part of your body that seems the most responsive or receptive to Mary's attitudes and emotions. Stay there until that experience begins to fade or is no longer as engaging. Then move your attention to another part . . . slowly . . . letting the experience sink in as deeply as possible. Perhaps after you have focused your attention once on her face, right hand and arm, left hand, breasts, and her feet and legs, you may find it effective to repeat the cycle one or several times, allowing the experience to be expanded or deepened.

During another prayer period, you may find it worthwhile to focus your attention on the crucified Jesus, similar to the way in which we considered the figure of Mary. You might consider Jesus as an image of your own crucified shadow child or of any part of your self that seems "dead." Slowly explore the figure of Jesus, taking on his emotions and attitudes as you perceive them. Be Jesus now, lying in Mary's arms. Look at Mary and receive her love and compassion, her nurturing and support.

It may be helpful to return occasionally to the Pieta in prayer. It may serve to bring forth or to deepen a needed inner reconciliation, and thus enable us to turn around and to rise to new life.

The Pieta gives a general circular impression, formed by Mary's open arms, her bowed head, and the curved body of Jesus. It suggests a wholeness that reinforces the deep reconciliation and reunion portrayed by the sculpture. The serenity of Mary's face and the repose of Jesus' face and body further strengthen the impression of wholeness. The battle is over. The foes within have been reconciled. There is peace. The ravages of war can be healed and creative activity can resume. Resurrection is possible and new life can begin.

Our inner child risen to new life is a joy and a delight. Let us take the hand of our beloved little child and let us celebrate together . . .

slumbering in the peace
   of a battle ended . . .
dreaming in the light
   of a shadow turned 'round . . .
waking to a new dawn
   with sight restored . . .
running with the freedom
   of a prisoner released . . .
skipping with the lightness
   of a burden lifted . . .
leaping with joy
   that the lost is found . . .
shouting with gladness
   at a treasure revealed . . .
hugging with the passion
   of a love renewed . . .
dancing to the rhythm
   of the Spirit of God . . .
singing the song
   of a soul set free . . .

Alleluia!
      Alleluia!
            Alleluia!